Knowing God and Having an Intimate Relationship with Him

by Dr. Anthony J. LuPardo

Words of Life Publications
Tulsa, Oklahoma

Knowing God and Having an
Intimate Relationship with Him
ISBN 0-9746038-0-5
Second Edition
Copyright © 2003 by
Dr. Anthony J. LuPardo
P. O. Box 54714
Tulsa, OK 74155
918/748-1777

Published by:

Words of Life Publications
P. O. Box 54714
Tulsa, OK 74155

Special Acknowledgments

First and foremost, I want to thank Almighty God, my Father; the Lord Jesus Christ, my best Friend; and my precious Friend, the Holy Spirit, for all they have been to me. I am eternally grateful that I have been saved, healed, and prospered through God's faithfulness and that He has spared my life and given me the privilege of writing this book. To Him be all the glory!

Next to Jesus I would like to thank my best friend and special partner, Gina, my precious wife of more than thirty years. I am so grateful for her love, encouragement, and prayers, without which this book would not have been possible.

I am also very grateful to my dearest daughter, Theresa Marie Stewart, my princess and encourager, whose love and care have strengthened me and given me great joy.

A very special thanks to the following people and organizations: To my editorial assistant, Marilyn Price, whose skillful help and dedication are most appreciated in making this book possible. To Pastor/Apostle Dr. Nike Daramy of Temple of Praise International Church, Beltsville,

Maryland, my spiritual daughter for her prayers, love, and financial support to help publish this book. To Pastors Ricky and Karla Musgrove of Faith Church, Edmond, Oklahoma, for their encouragement and financial support to publish this book. To Pastors Murray and Serena Blurton, longtime friends and faithful ministry partners. To Pastors Bob and Willa Williams, longtime faithful partners.

I am also deeply grateful, humbled, and honored by my special friends, Jeff and Susan Davis, and DSE Technologies, whose constant encouragement and financial support have made this book a reality.

I thank God for all of these wonderful people He has placed in my life to pray for me and who have contributed to the success of this book. I especially thank God for my sister Carrie who prayed us into the Kingdom of God; my spiritual Momma in the Lord, Evangelist Christine V. Johnson, whose love, friendship, and encouragement in the Lord have been most gratifying. She has been a wonderful example to my wife and me;

and my two sisters in the Lord and intercessors, Peggy Talley and Nellie Livingston, whose prayers have deeply affected my life and ministry.

Above all, my sincere thanks to God for the opportunity to share this message of intimacy with Him.

Contents

Foreword

The Lord spoke to my heart and said, "Son, you need no man or person to write the foreword for this book. It is My doing and it is marvelous in My sight. This book was given by My Holy Spirit for the benefit of My believers, the Church, and all the world, so they may come to know Me and have an intimate relationship with Me. I will get all the glory. My blessings upon those who read this book and put it into practice."

Agape,

God Almighty

Preface

My purpose for writing this book is motivated by my lifelong quest to know God. In that regard, I have endeavored to share about knowing God and having an intimate relationship (*ginosko* in Greek) with Him.

To know God and to have an intimate relationship with Him is based upon a daily experiential relationship with Him. It takes a daily seeking of Him through His Word, through prayer, and by fellowship with the Holy Spirit to produce that union with Him.

Indeed, knowing God comes only by revelation of the Holy Spirit, and it comes in various forms through daily experiences so that as you seek Him through your everyday life, you will find Him. Actually, the truth of the matter is, He is seeking you – daily!

God's greatest desire is to have an intimate relationship with you. God wants to reveal

Himself to His people in these last days as never before. We are living in a prophetic time set aside by God to reveal Himself to the world, to His Church, and to His people individually. What an exciting time to be alive and to know Him!

It is my sincere and heartfelt prayer that as you read this book it will create a lifelong hunger in your heart, a stir in your spirit, and a thirst in your soul to know God intimately.

Dr. Anthony J. LuPardo

Chapter 1

Entryway to Knowing God

I was sitting in my car one day at the beach in Redondo Beach, California. It was a beautiful fall day and the sunset was magnificent – blue skies and gently rolling waves, not a cloud in the sky, cool breeze, and everything that should make life happy – but here I was contemplating suicide.

My life had been failing miserably. I had experienced great success in my early years in business, being a young executive in Europe for my company which I had administrated. I had acquired several million dollar contracts and enjoyed living in the fast lane. But even then with great accomplishments and success, my life seemed very empty. I kept myself occupied and consumed with work and entertainment to fill the void.

But now my business success was gone, my marriage was failing, I was supernaturally in debt, and life seemed fruitless with no way out. I had come to the ocean to seek a way out of all my problems and troubles. Still with all the beauty around me in this wonderful California setting, there were no answers, so I was deeply contemplating suicide day after day.

Finally, one evening while watching TV, I saw a man giving his testimony about entering in to knowing God. I was real interested in listening to this man, whom I knew about, as he was the vice president of Lear Jet Corporation. He had many airplane inventions and great success in the aircraft field, which I was a part of and spent twenty-five plus years of my life in both aviation and in the military.

I listened to him very intently as he described his successes and failures and how he learned about the entryway to knowing God, which turned his life around.

At that moment, I got down on my knees and prayed to know God. Immediately the desire to commit suicide left me, and peace and joy flooded my soul.

My problems weren't immediately solved, but I did find the answers and each challenge was turned into victory. That's why I believe this book will help you to know Him and gain insights for your own life.

In Matthew's gospel we find Jesus crying out and saying, *Come unto me, all ye that labour and are heavy laden, and I will give you rest. Take my yoke upon you, and learn of me; for I am meek and lowly in heart: and ye shall find rest unto your souls* (Matthew 11:28-29 KJV).

The only entryway to knowing God is through Jesus Christ, His Son.

Do you know that the only burden Jesus places on you is to know Him? "Come and learn of Me." That's the only burden you will ever have.

Consequently, there is only one way that you can know God. The only entryway to knowing Him is through Jesus Christ, His Son. In John 14:6 KJV Jesus says, *I am the way, the truth, and the life: no man cometh unto the Father, but by me.*

Nicodemus, a Sinner, Comes to Jesus

John 3:1-2 KJV introduces us to Nicodemus: *There was a man of the Pharisees, named Nicodemus, a ruler of the Jews: The same came to Jesus by night, and said unto him, Rabbi, we know that thou art a teacher come from God: for no man can do these miracles that thou doest, except God be with him.*

"Except a man be born again, he cannot see the kingdom of God" (John 3:3 KJV).

Nicodemus was acknowledging that Jesus knew God because of the miracles He did. And in his heart he wanted to know God too. So he bypassed the religious rhetoric of the day and came to Jesus.

This passage continues, *Jesus answered and said unto him, Verily, verily, I say unto thee, Except a man be born again, he cannot see the kingdom of God. Nicodemus saith unto him, How can a man be born when he is old? can he enter the second time into his mother's womb, and be born? Jesus answered, Verily, verily, I say unto thee, Except a man be born of water and of the Spirit, he cannot enter into the kingdom of*

God. That which is born of the flesh is flesh; and that which is born of the Spirit is spirit (John 3:3-6 KJV).

In this passage of Scripture, Jesus is describing to Nicodemus the entryway to knowing God. To know God you must be born again. John 3:16 KJV says, *For God so loved the world, that he gave his only begotten Son, that whosoever believeth in him should not perish, but have everlasting life.* Clearly, we see here that the way to knowing God then and entering into the Kingdom of God is through the born-again experience, making Jesus the Lord of your life.

Romans 10:8-10 tells us exactly how we can know God. We are saved and become children of God through Jesus Christ's sacrifice for us. The way of salvation is described in Romans 10:9,10: *If you confess with your mouth the Lord Jesus and believe in your heart that God has raised Him from the dead, you will be saved. For with the heart one believes unto righteousness, and with the mouth confession is made unto salvation.*

> **"If you confess with your mouth the Lord Jesus and believe in your heart that God has raised Him from the dead, you will be saved" (Romans 10:9).**

If you've never done that, today is your day of salvation. Just ask Jesus to come into your heart and be the Lord of your life. Pray this prayer with me out loud right now from your heart.

Say:

> *Father, I believe that Jesus Christ is Your Son, and that He was crucified, buried, and resurrected to provide a way of salvation/exchange for me. When I accept Him as my Lord and Savior, He forgives all of my sins, forgets all of my past, and gives me righteousness for my unrighteousness. He gives me health, wholeness, and well-being for sickness and disease. He provides abundance for lack and eternal life in exchange for eternal damnation. Right now, Jesus, come into my heart and be my Lord and Savior. It's a new day for me because You shed Your blood for me, and I receive that costly sacrifice! Amen.*

You have gained eternal life. This is the entryway to knowing God. Now you can begin to have an intimate relationship with God.

Ephesians 2:7-8 says, *That in the ages to come He might show the exceeding riches of His grace in His kindness toward us in Christ Jesus. For by grace you have been saved through faith, and that not of yourselves; it is the gift of God.*

You see, salvation is a free gift to those who

Accepting Jesus Christ as your Lord and Savior is the entryway to knowing God.

will receive it. You don't have to do anything to earn it.

It doesn't come by being good or doing good works. It is through grace alone that you receive new life in Jesus Christ. It is the grace of God in manifestation on your behalf through the cross of the Lord Jesus Christ. It is the means of salvation by which God forgives all of your sins and accepts you into His Kingdom.

Just come to Him as you are, in faith, believing in Him and confessing Him as Lord of your life. He will accept you and transform you.

Many of us have, in fact, received Jesus into our hearts and have confessed Him as Lord of our lives, and we have entered into the Kingdom of God. But that's only the first step in knowing Him. We can come into a continuous daily intimate relationship with Him through prayer and reading His Word, which I will describe in the chapters that follow.

It is through grace alone, not by works or good deeds, that you receive new life in Jesus Christ.

Chapter 2

Empowered to Know God

The empowerment for knowing God comes from the Holy Spirit by revelation. The Holy Sprit is the great Revelator. He reveals God the Father to us and He reveals Jesus to us. However, you must enter into the revelation of the Holy Spirit by faith. By studying and meditating on God's Word and through prayer, God will reveal Himself to us. It takes a daily application of Bible reading and communion with God in prayer in order to have an intimate relationship with Him.

As we look at some scriptures, we will discover the power of God is needed to receive the revelation of God. In Luke 24:49 Jesus says, *Behold, I send the Promise of My Father upon you; but tarry in the city of Jerusalem until you are endued with power from on high.*

> **So Jesus sends the promise of the Father, which is the Holy Spirit, that we might be gifted with God's power, which will enable us to know Him.**

The word "endued" in this scripture means to be gifted with power or gifted with God's power for knowing Him. The word "power" in this scripture is the word *dunamis* where we get the English word "dynamite." So Jesus sends the promise of the Father, which is the Holy Spirit, that we might be gifted with God's power, which will enable us to know Him.

Acts 1:8 tells us, *But you shall receive power* [dunamis] *when the Holy Spirit has come upon you; and you shall be witnesses to Me in Jerusalem, and in all Judea and Samaria, and to the end of the earth.*

This power was poured out on the day of Pentecost, and that same power of the Holy Spirit is here today to reveal God and Christ to us. Acts

2:1-4 tells us, *Now when the Day of Pentecost had fully come, they were all with one accord in one place. And suddenly there came a sound from heaven, as of a rushing mighty wind, and it filled the whole house where they were sitting. Then there* **The Holy Spirit fully came on the day of Pentecost, and He is still fully here and available today.** *appeared to them divided tongues, as of fire, and one sat upon each of them. And they were all filled with the Holy Spirit and began to speak with other tongues, as the Spirit gave them utterance.*

So you see, on the day of Pentecost the Holy Spirit had fully come. He was fully poured out so that we might have an intimate relationship with God.

In Luke 11:13 Jesus says that if a natural father knows how to give good gifts to his children, how much more will the heavenly Father give the Holy Spirit to those who ask Him. So you see, if we ask the heavenly Father for the precious Holy Spirit, He will empower us to know Him.

Empowerment by God then is a must for having an intimate relationship with Him. The Christian who tries to know God and live the Christian life in his own strength will simply fail because it takes the power of God to live the Christian life and to know Him.

> **If a natural father knows how to give good gifts to his children, how much more will the heavenly Father give the Holy Spirit to those who ask Him.**

The power of the Holy Spirit, which was given on the day of Pentecost, was not solely designed for the first century Church. Rather, all Christians are indwelt by the Holy Spirit and, therefore, have His power available.

The believer must live the Christian life daily, but he does it successfully through the empowerment of the Holy Spirit. Described practically, the believer must appropriate the Holy Spirit to assist in Christian living and knowing God daily by faith. It is a simple reliance on the Holy Spirit to help reveal God to the believer by faith daily.

So to have that intimate relationship with God and that steadfast walk with Jesus Christ, you need to call upon the precious Holy Spirit and ask Him to empower you.

Remember, you cannot live an overcoming Christian life alone. It takes the Holy Spirit, that Great Revelator, to give you revelation of who God is, and what He wants to be to you and in you and for you so that you may have an intimate relationship with Him. Learn to ask

It takes the power of God to live the Christian life and to know Him.

the Holy Spirit for His guidance in your daily Bible reading and prayer life so that you can develop that intimate relationship with the Father, the Son, and the Holy Spirit.

Chapter 3

Revelation to Know God Comes by Faith

There's only one way you can come to God and get to know Him and that is by faith. The only way you can experience His righteousness and intimacy is through faith. Hebrews 11:6 tells us, *But without faith it is impossible to please Him, for he who comes to God must believe that He is, and that He is a rewarder of those who diligently seek Him.*

> "He who comes to God must believe that He is, and that He is a rewarder of those who diligently seek Him" (Hebrews 11:6).

One day the Lord spoke to me about this scripture from Hebrews 11:6. He said to me, "I'm a rewarder of those who diligently seek Me." He said it again, "I'm a rewarder of those who diligently seek Me." I said, "Yes, Lord." He spoke a third time, "I said I'm a rewarder of those who diligently seek Me."

"Do you know what My reward is to you for diligently seeking Me?"

I responded abruptly, almost annoyed, "Yes, Lord, why are You telling me that?"

Then He spoke very softly and said, using *King James* English, "Wherefore thou can I reward thee except with that which I am?" I said, "What?" He said it again, "Wherefore thou can I reward thee except with that which I am?" I said, "What?" He repeated it a third time, this time in a stronger tone, "Wherefore thou can I reward thee except with that which I am?" I responded, "What are You trying to say to me, Lord?" He was using *King James* English, and that's why I know it was the Lord, because I'm not very fond of *King James* English and I don't have a very keen understanding of it.

The Lord then responded to me and said, "Do you know what My reward is to you for diligently seeking Me?" I said, "No, Lord. What is it?"

He said, "My reward, son, for those who diligently seek Me is more of Myself." I said, "What?" He repeated it, "My reward for those who diligently seek Me is more of Myself."

I said, "Oh, Father, Lord Jesus, I'm hungry for You. I will diligently seek You more and more from now on. Amen."

Ever since that day, it has been part of my quest to diligently seek Him and have the intimate relationship with Him daily so that He might reward me with more of Himself. How about you? Are you hungry enough to diligently seek Him daily? He will reward you with more of Himself! Praise God!

> He said, "My reward for those who diligently seek Me is more of Myself."

Hebrews 11:6 tells us that not only must you believe that God exists, you must believe that He will reward you if you diligently seek Him. God's reward to you for diligently seeking Him is a greater and more intimate relationship with Him. This relationship is ongoing and it is continually established by faith. It's what I call *the great exchange*. As you pour out your heart to God in prayer and seek

Him through His Word, He will exchange with you His love, His character, and all that He is. If you continue to seek Him, the end result will be an ever-increasing intimate relationship with Him.

So you see, it takes faith to please God and faith to know Him intimately. Romans 12:3 says, *For I say, through the grace given to me, to everyone who is among you, not to think of himself more highly than he ought to think but to think soberly, as God has dealt to each one a measure of faith.*

Every person — every man, woman, and child — has been given a measure of faith. But if you don't choose to believe God's Word and exercise the faith you already have, you won't come to know Him or have an intimate relationship with Him.

God is prophetically calling mankind, especially believers, unto Himself to have an ever-increasing intimate relationship with Him.

God desires believers who are already in the Kingdom to turn wholeheartedly to Him.

In the earth then God is moving on the hearts of man. He desires souls to come into His

Kingdom, but He also desires believers who are already in the Kingdom to turn wholeheartedly to Him.

The Wise and Foolish Virgins

Let's look at the story of the ten virgins in Matthew 25:1-13. In this passage we see the parable of Jesus dealing with the ten virgins, five of whom were wise and maintained their oil (intimate relationship with God), and five who were foolish and were without oil and did not maintain that relationship. We see the results of maintaining this relationship or not maintaining it.

Let's look at the scripture and then you make your own decision as to the worth of having that daily intimate relationship with Him.

1   *"Then the kingdom of heaven shall be likened to ten virgins who took their lamps and went out to meet the bridegroom.*

2   *"Now five of them were wise, and five were foolish.*

3   *"Those who were foolish took their lamps
     and took no oil with them,*

4   *"but the wise took oil in their vessels with
     their lamps.*

5   *"But while the bridegroom was delayed,
     they all slumbered and slept.*

6   *"And at midnight a cry was heard:
     'Behold, the bridegroom is coming; go out to
     meet him!'*

7   *"Then all those virgins arose and trimmed
     their lamps.*

8   *"And the foolish said to the wise, 'Give us
     some of your oil, for our lamps are going
     out.'*

9   *"But the wise answered, saying, 'No, lest
     there should not be enough for us and you;
     but go rather to those who sell, and buy
     for yourselves.'*

10   *"And while they went to buy, the bride-
     groom came, and those who were ready
     went in with him to the wedding; and the
     door was shut.*

11   *"Afterward the other virgins came also, say-
     ing, 'Lord, Lord, open to us!'*

12   *"But he answered and said, 'Assuredly, I
     say to you, I do not know you.'*

13   *"Watch therefore, for you know neither the*
day nor the hour in which the Son of Man
is coming."

In this parable the ten virgins were all believers. They were all waiting for the bridegroom but they didn't all have oil. Five of them had oil, and five of them didn't. The oil represents the Holy Spirit and an ongoing relationship with God. This parable talks about five virgins who were wise and five virgins who were foolish. The wise had oil in their vessels, which means they had that ongoing presence of God. The foolish ones slumbered and slept and did not cultivate the oil of the Spirit, or their ongoing relationship with God.

Again, verses 8 and 9 say:

8   *"And the foolish said to the wise, 'Give us*
some of your oil, for our lamps are going out.'
9   *"But the wise answered, saying, 'No, lest there*
should not be enough for us and you; but go
rather to those who sell, and buy for
yourselves.'"

I want you to notice that in this passage of Scripture the wise virgins had the oil of the Spirit, which comes from having a growing, intimate relationship with God, while the foolish virgins did not have that perpetual relationship. Therefore, they were out of oil and needed to go out to acquire some. Had they maintained their intimate relationship with God, the foolish virgins would not have had to go out and acquire their oil at the time when the King was coming. (We do not know precisely when midnight will come.)

The wise virgins had the oil of the Spirit, which comes from having a growing, intimate relationship with God.

Verse 10 says that while they went to acquire the oil, or stir up that relationship, the bridegroom came. Those who were ready and had the oil, or the relationship, went in to the wedding feast and the door was shut behind them. But the other five virgins who went to reacquire oil, when they came back, they cried, "Lord, Lord, open the door to us." But He answered, *Assuredly, I say to you, I do not know you.*

God's warning in verse 13 is, *Watch, therefore, for you know neither the day nor the hour in which the Son of Man is coming.* This is a sad condition in which to find yourself.

The *Ginosko* Relationship

When Jesus said in verse 12, "Depart from Me. I do not know you," the word "know" in the Greek is the word *ginosko*, which means "I never had an intimate relationship with you." Now when Paul in his writings to the Philippians in chapter 3, verse 10, cries out to know God, it's also that same Greek word *ginosko*. And in Luke 1:34, Mary said to the angel, as he informed her that she would have a child who would be the Messiah and that she should call His name Jesus, *How can this be, since I do not know a man?* This word "know" in the Greek is the same word *ginosko*.

This word *ginosko* in *Vine's Expository Dictionary*, describes having an intimate relationship such as marriage or intercourse, a union that ends in euphoria and ecstasy. This is the same term that Paul uses in reference to knowing Him in Philippians 3:10, and it's the same word that Jesus uses in Matthew 25:12 and in Luke 1:34 with Mary. God is not talking about sex when He uses the term *ginosko*. He is talking about an intimate relationship that ends in ecstasy and euphoria which comes only through knowing Him.

You see, the parable of the virgins describes our marriage union with the Bridegroom, and that union should be cultivated daily in our lives.

Ginosko – to know God – is the key to intimacy.

Having that special relationship with Him should be our utmost quest. It should be a heartfelt hunger after God that is established in joy and ends in ecstasy and euphoria. We will talk more about this *ginosko* relationship that Paul had in a later chapter.

There are many churchgoers and believers today who are in the same condition as the foolish virgins were. They know about God. They have come to Jesus and received Him as Lord, but they do not live in the Spirit or have this ongoing *ginosko* (intimate relationship) with Him. So eventually they turn cold.

But the Bridegroom will come to seek us out, and those of us who maintain our oil – the oil of joy, the oil of gladness, the oil of the flow of His presence in an intimate relationship with Him –

will go in and have that intimate relationship forever. To God be the glory!

However, to those who do not maintain their oil, or intimate relationship with Him, He will say, "Be gone from Me. I do not know you." In other words, "You've never had that heartfelt relationship with Me that ends in ecstasy and euphoria."

God is looking for us as believers to hunger and thirst after Him and have that heartfelt relationship with Him on a daily basis.

> **Vine describes *ginosko* as having an intimate relationship . . . a union that ends in euphoria and ecstasy.**

Chapter 4

Intimacy with God Versus Acquaintanceship

There is NOTHING more important in your life than knowing God Almighty. Not your job, your finances, your children, or even your spouse. Therefore, knowing God should be the number one priority in your daily life.

There is a vast difference between intimacy and acquaintanceship. Intimacy involves spending deep heartfelt personal time – a time so special as to bear your whole heart and soul to that other person to give of your entire being. This is what it takes to have that intimate relationship with God, communicating with Him with all of your being, pouring your heart out to

Him, lavishing Him with your love and thanksgiving for who He is and what He has done for you in Jesus Christ.

On the other hand, acquaintanceship is just a casual knowing about someone and never becoming intimate with them. Unfortunately, many believers have God as an acquaintance but never really enter into that deep intimacy with Him, which He so desires.

Knowing God should be the number one priority in your daily life.

He loves you so much He paid the supreme price, sending Jesus to the cross to redeem you back to Himself in order for you to have intimacy with Him. Selah.

But you can't really know God if you don't have an intimate relationship with Him. That requires spending time with Him to build that relationship. We all have friends and family we know intimately, and then there are other people who are just acquaintances. The Lord once said to me, "Anthony, so many of My people don't really know Me. I'm like an acquaintance to them.

They stay so busy that they do not spend quality time with Me."

God was saying that there are people who know about Him but they do not have that deep, intimate relationship with Him. Their relationship with Him is just as an acquaintance. There is a great difference between these two types of relationships.

For example, a relationship based upon acquaintance is one of casual contact and not necessarily one of intimacy, or just a passing friendship. A relationship of intimacy, however, requires time to develop and is an exchange of very deep heartfelt care and feeling. An intimate relationship involves the emergence of your entire being. In other words, it's spirit, soul, and body yielded to God from a heart of thanksgiving and gratefulness as to who He is and the great things He has done. The development of this relationship again requires spending quality time with Him.

As previously mentioned, before you can have an intimate relationship with the living God, you must accept Jesus Christ as your Lord and Savior. (See Romans 10:9-10.) This is the initial introduction to knowing Him.

The Holy Spirit reveals the subsequent development of that relationship to you in an ongoing, ever-increasing manner as you enter into the process of seeking God daily. He will lead you into that intimate relationship that you desire with God.

Great Exploits for Those Who Know Him

If you desire to accomplish much for God in your life and do great exploits for Him, then you must cultivate this intimate, daily relationship in order to have the wisdom, power, and might to accomplish all that He has for you.

> **An intimate relationship involves the emergence of your entire being – spirit, soul, and body – yielded to God from a heart of thanksgiving and gratefulness.**

All of the biblical scholars agree that we are living in the last days, and God is crying out for His people to come to Him. He is saying, *The people that do know their God shall be strong, and do exploits* (Daniel 11:32 KJV). If you want to know

God and be strong and do exploits in these last days, you must have that intimate relationship with Him on a regular basis.

Knowing the living God, then, should not only be our number one priority but our utmost goal. We should desire to know Him in all of **Knowing God should be our utmost goal.**

His glory. That means we should know His character, His nature, and His very being.

Cultivating an Intimate Relationship

The Bible tells us that God is love. His very essence is love (*agape* or unconditional love). As we read and study His Word and experience answered prayer, we begin to know Him, trust Him, believe in Him, and have faith in Him.

Desire to know Him in all His glory, knowing His character, His nature, and His very being.

Further intimate relationship with God comes through worship and praise. There is a vast difference between worship and praise. When we worship God we are to worship Him in spirit and in truth. We worship Him for who He is, but praise is different. Praise is for His actions – for what He has done, for what He is doing, and for what He is going to do.

Reading the Word daily, praying, and meditating upon God's Word, worshipping and praising Him, is how you cultivate that intimate relationship.

Relationship or Religion?

There is a vast difference between religion and relationship. Religion is having a form of godliness but denying its power (2 Timothy 3:5). Religion knows about God but doesn't have the intimate relationship with God.

> **There is a vast difference between religion and relationship.**

Above everything, religion has taught us to be afraid of God. Religion is of the devil because it glorifies man and his works instead of glorifying God. Jesus hated religion for this reason, and the religious leaders were scorned by Him because they did not know God or accept Him as Messiah.

They thought their good works were enough to please God and have a relationship with Him, but they were not, because you cannot know God through good works. You can only know Him through a heart-felt relationship with Him.

Religion glorifies man, not God.

There were many religious practices in Jesus' day that were strictly of a spiritual nature wherein they did good works, but they did not develop a heartfelt relationship toward God or their fellowman. This is also true today.

Relationship is much different than *religion* in that first and foremost, you have an intimate relationship with God, with Jesus,

You cannot know God through good works. You can only know Him through a heart-felt relationship with Him.

and with the Holy Spirit. Out of that relationship you are created to do good works toward your fellowman and to glorify God. This type of relationship is pleasing to God, for you have been created for good works in Christ Jesus that are not solely a religious practice, but are formed from your heartfelt relationship with God.

Chapter 5

Paul Hungered to Know God

Paul desired to know God. He yearned for an intimate relationship with Him. At the end of his ministry as he was about to sacrifice his life and go on to be with the Lord, even at that point Paul was crying out to know Him.

In reviewing the Scriptures, we see the Apostle Paul's hunger for knowing God. We must realize that Paul **Paul cries out to know Him more.** wrote a majority of the New Testament by revelation, yet he was crying out to know Him more. This really tells us something. Paul had great revelation or knowledge of His Word, but he desired to have an ever-increasing fellowship with Him.

Let's look at the Scriptures as Paul endeavors to satisfy this hunger.

In Philippians 3:7-15 Paul writes:

7 *But what things were gain to me, these I have counted loss for Christ.*

8 *Yet indeed I also count all things loss for the excellence of the knowledge of Christ Jesus my Lord, for whom I have suffered the loss of all things, and count them as rubbish, that I may gain Christ*

9 *and be found in Him, not having my own righteousness, which is from the law, but that which is through faith in Christ, the righteousness which is from God by faith;*

10 *that I may know Him and the power of His resurrection, and the fellowship of His sufferings, being conformed to His death,*

The whole emphasis of the book of Philippians is Paul's statement, "That I may know Him . . ." (Philippians 3:10).

11 *if, by any means, I may attain to the resurrection from the dead.*

12 *Not that I have already attained, or am already perfected; but I press on, that I may lay hold of that for which Christ Jesus has also laid hold of me.*

13 *Brethren, I do not count myself to have apprehended; but one thing I do, forgetting those things which are behind and reaching forward to those things which are ahead,*

14 *I press toward the goal for the prize of the upward call of God in Christ Jesus.*

15 *Therefore let us, as many as are mature, have this mind....*

Let's review. In verse 7 Paul says, *But what things were gain to me, these I have counted loss for Christ.* In verses 8 and 9 he says, *Yet indeed I also count all things loss for the excellence of the knowledge of Christ Jesus my Lord, for whom I have suffered the loss of all things, and count them as rubbish, that I may gain*

> **"I press toward the goal for the prize of the upward call of God in Christ Jesus"** (Philippians 3:14).

Christ, and be found in Him, not having my own righteousness, which is from the law, but that which is through faith in Christ, the righteousness which is from God by faith.

There is no greater possession than to know Him!

What was Paul saying? In verse 7 he was saying that everything he had gained — his worldly possessions, his high position as a Pharisee (obviously he had great success in life and fame and fortune among his peers), "I count everything [note that he said "everything"] as loss for the excellence of the knowledge of Christ Jesus my Lord." He considered all the things that he had gained as rubbish compared to knowing Christ.

Verse 9 indicates that Paul desired to be found in Christ, not having his own righteousness which was from the law, but being righteous in Christ through faith which is from God.

Paul considered all the things that he had gained as rubbish compared to knowing Christ.

Notice that as we come to Christ through faith in God, we are no longer righteous in our own abilities or strengths, but we have been made the righteousness of God in Christ Jesus. A large part of our intimate relationship with Him is based upon the righteousness that is ours through Christ. It is that intimacy with God that Paul desired so dearly that he was willing to sacrifice everything for it.

In verses 10 and 11 Paul cries out, *That I may know Him and the power of His resurrection, and the fellowship of His sufferings, being conformed to His death, if, by any means, I may attain to the resurrection from the dead.*

A *Ginosko* Relationship of Ecstasy and Euphoria

In verse 10, the phrase "that I may **know** Him" is where we get the word *ginosko*. As I stated previously, in *Vine's Expository Dictionary ginosko* has a meaning of intimate relationship like unto the marriage union. It actually means a relationship that ends in ecstasy and euphoria. It is a relationship like unto sexual intercourse.

> **Ginosko is the key to knowing Him.**

Sexual intercourse is not a bad term, but it has been perverted by the world, the devil, and the flesh. God designed sexual intercourse for marriage. It was His intent that the marriage union bring glory to God and build family relationships. In that regard, this intimate relationship is much more than just physical. It is first and foremost a heart relationship. It is a spiritual relationship first with God from the heart. And then it becomes beneficial to husband and wife and family.

God describes this marriage relationship very well in the book of Song of Songs. This is what *ginosko* means: God first in that intimate relationship and then man and his family having that intimate relationship together. So many marriages and families fail because they do not seek God first with all of their hearts and have that *ginosko* with Him;

> **Your intimate relationship with God will overflow spirit, soul, and body and bless everyone around you.**

i.e., euphoria and ecstasy in prayer and praise. Therefore, that intimate relationship with the spouse, family, and others is not present. This is what is missing and leads to failure in most families.

As you learn to develop this intimate relationship from your heart with God, then **Paul was willing to pay any price to know Christ.** that heartfelt relationship will be poured out on everyone around you. In other words, your intimate relationship with God will overflow spirit, soul, and body and bless everyone around you. That's why this intimate relationship is so important. *Paul knew that. That's why he was crying out for this type of relationship with God* even at the end of his career. Paul even cried out to know Him and the power of His resurrection and the fellowship of His sufferings, being conformed to His death.

If you study this out in the Greek, you will find that Paul wanted to know Christ so much that he even desired, if it were possible, to experience what Jesus experienced in His death on the cross, so that he might know Him. That's a whole lot of knowing, don't you think?

Shouldn't we want to know Him as much as Paul did? Paul wrote two-thirds of the New Testament, yet we see in the Scriptures that he was still crying out to know Him. So this should be our heartfelt cry as well.

We should be willing to pay any price to know Christ, just as Paul did.

Paul says in verse 12, *Not that I have already attained, or am already perfected; but I press on, that I may lay hold of that for which Christ Jesus has also laid hold of me.*

Verses 13 and 14 tell us, *Brethren, I do not count myself to have apprehended* [obtained]; *but one thing I do, forgetting those things which are behind* [past] *and reaching* [or stretching] *forward to those things which are ahead, I press toward the goal* [or the mark] *for the prize of the upward call of God in Christ Jesus.*

If Paul hadn't arrived, then we haven't either!

Paul is saying in these verses that he has not arrived, he has not attained, nor is he perfected in this *ginosko* [intimate relationship], but he gives us a clue here on how to acquire it. He says in verses 13 and 14 that he forgets the things which are past and he stretches or presses forward to those things which are ahead.

So the key to building this intimate relationship with God is forgetting and pressing — *forgetting* and *pressing*. That's Paul's answer to building his intimate relation-

> **The key to building this intimate relationship with God is forgetting and pressing.**

ship with his Lord. Now we should do the same. Forget the past, whether it be your successes, your failures, your offenses, or your bad relationships. Forsake the past and press on into God daily to have this intimate relationship with Him.

Pressing Forward for a Prize

Paul tells us that he pressed toward the mark for the prize of the high calling of God in Christ Jesus. Notice what he said here. He was pressing forward for a prize.

As you study this in the Greek, the way it is written is like unto a Greek Olympic runner who is running a race for a prize. Gaining the prize is his ultimate goal, much like one of our athletes would run for a gold medal in an Olympic competition today.

Knowing Christ is our greatest prize.

But the prize, the greatest prize of all for winning this race that Paul talked about, it's Christ Jesus Himself — that intimate, euphoric ecstasy in our relationship with God. Praise God! What a prize!

In verse 15 Paul admonishes us, *As many as are mature, have this mind.* . . . Are you mature? Do you want to be mature? You must have this mind-set to have this intimate relationship with God. That's what Paul was saying.

My heartfelt cry is for you to have this intimate relationship with God.

After reading this passage, I recommend that you search your heart to see where you are with God, and cry out to Him to give you this kind of relationship. It is my fervent prayer that God will reveal Himself to you in this intimate and very special way on a daily basis.

Chapter 6

Knowing God the Father

In our quest for an intimate relationship with God, we must know God as Father, we must know Jesus as Lord, and we must know the Holy Spirit. Described practically, we must have a relationship with the full Godhead in order to have an intimate relationship with God.

We are not speaking of three Gods. But we are speaking of three persons in one God. They are the Father, the Son, and the Holy Ghost. They are three individual persons but one and the same God. I don't endeavor to understand completely the Godhead, but I do understand that they are one and the same God but three different persons and, therefore, I desire that you may know each one of them individually.

In further trying to understand the Godhead, I find that we

God is three persons in one God.

as humans are three-part beings. Each of us has been made spirit, soul, and body, yet we are one and the same person. Through this example, I have come to understand the Godhead. With that in mind, in the next few chapters we will look at knowing God the Father, knowing God the Son, and

Each of us has been made spirit, soul, and body, yet we are one and the same person.

knowing God the Holy Spirit so we can learn how to have an intimate relationship with Him.

Jesus and the Father Are One

Knowing God the Father begins with accepting Jesus Christ as your Lord and Savior. In John 14:6-11 Jesus said:

6   *Jesus said to him, "I am the way, the truth, and the life. No one comes to the Father except through Me.*

7   *"If you had known Me, you would have known My Father also; and from now on you know Him and have seen Him."*

8   *Philip said to Him, "Lord, show us the Father, and it is sufficient for us."*

9   *Jesus said to him, "Have I been with you so long, and yet you have not known Me, Philip? He who has seen Me has seen the Father; so how can you say, 'Show us the Father'?*

10 *"Do you not believe that I am in the Father, and the Father in Me? The words that I speak to you I do not speak on My own authority; but the Father who dwells in Me does the works.*

11 *"Believe Me that I am in the Father and the Father in Me, or else believe Me for the sake of the works themselves."*

So we see in these verses that Jesus and the Father are in union. They are one. Jesus said to Philip in verse 9, *He who has seen Me has seen the Father; so how can you say, "Show us the Father"?* So we see here the union of God the Father and Christ Jesus the Son. They are one.

Accepting Jesus then as your Lord and Savior is your introduction to the Father. The

Holy Spirit draws you to repentance so that you can receive Jesus, and Jesus introduces you to the Father when you accept the work of the cross and confess Him as Lord.

Abiding in Love

In order to have this intimate relationship with God, you must understand and believe by faith that God loves you so much that He sacrificed His Son Jesus to prove and to manifest His love to you!!!

God loves you unconditionally in spite of your sins, your failures, and your shortcomings. He gives you unconditional love when you accept Jesus as your Lord and Savior.

From knowing this and believing by faith in His love for you, is how you will build an intimate relationship with Him and grow in it.

Love is the whole basis of your intimate relationship with God and with your fellowman.

Many Christians never enter into this relationship because they don't understand how much God loves them, and they never enter into all God has for them by faith in His love for them.

Therefore, I highly recommend that you study the scriptures in the book of First John, and as you study them, ask God to give you a revelation of His love for you!

Jesus' whole purpose is to introduce and establish our relationship with God our Father. First John 4:15-16 says, *Whoever confesses that Jesus is the Son of God, God abides in him, and he in God. And we have known and believed the love that God has for us. God is love, and he who abides in love abides in God, and God in him.*

Romans 5:5 tells us that the love of God has been shed abroad in our hearts by the Holy Spirit. So Jesus introduces us to God the Father who is love. Then the Holy Spirit comes and reveals the Father in us and to us.

God Showed Me His Love

One day after being discharged from the hospital suffering from a major heart attack, which brought me within a hair's breath of death, I was attending Prayer and Healing School at a major college in Tulsa.

While sitting there listening to the scriptures on healing, I felt like death warmed over and was ready to give up.

> **"God is love, and he who abides in love abides in God, and God in him" (1 John 4:16).**

God spoke to my heart and said, "Son, if you only knew and understood My love for you, through Jesus Christ's suffering on the cross, you would receive a new heart right now!"

As the instructor was explaining the scriptures on how by Jesus' stripes I was healed (1 Peter 2:24; Isaiah 53:4-5; Matthew 8:17; Exodus 15:26), I began to weep. I felt God's love for me in a dimension that I never knew before. I went forward for prayer right then and received a brand-new heart. To God be all the glory!

Most people, however, never enter into the fullness of all of God's promises and blessings because they don't fully

> **Most people never enter the fullness of God's love.**

understand God's love for them at the point of their need.

Knowing God in Spirit and in Truth

John 4:24 says, *God is Spirit, and those who worship Him must worship in spirit and truth.* So to know God the Father and have that intimate relationship with Him, we must worship Him in spirit and in truth. Worshipping God in spirit means that we worship Him for who He is. He is God Almighty, the one and only God, Creator of all the uni-

> **Worshipping God in spirit means that we worship Him for who He is.**

verse. There is no other God but Him. He alone is God. He is Jehovah, the God of Abraham, Isaac, and Jacob, the Father of our Lord Jesus Christ. Hallelujah!

Romans 8:15 says that we can call Him "Abba, Father," which means Daddy-God. If we have been born again, then He is truly our very own Father. We are to worship Him with all our spirit, soul (which includes the mind, will, and emotions), and body. This is the first commandment – that we love Him with all our being.

We love Him through worship and praise. Worship and praise and our prayer life are some of the key ways to build our intimate relationship with the Father.

Another way that's mentioned in Scripture is knowing Him in truth. Jesus says in John 17:17 KJV, *Thy word is truth*. So speaking the Word back to God in prayer is another way of having an intimate relationship with Him. God the Father only understands two things:

> **Worship and praise and our prayer life are some of the key ways to build our intimate relationship with the Father.**

your worship and praise, and speaking the Word back to Him. This is knowing God in spirit and in truth. And this is what will build your intimate relationship with Him.

To know God the Father then we must read and study and meditate upon His Word. The Old Testament reveals to us God the Father. It reveals to us His nature, His character, His person, His commands, and His will, as well as the

> **Speaking the Word back to God in prayer is another way of having an intimate relationship with Him.**

great and mighty things He has done and desires to do.

The Holy Spirit, who is the author of all Scripture, gives us a very vivid picture of the Father in the Old Testament – who He is and what He desires to be to us. He is Almighty God, a loving Father, who loved us so much that He gave His only begotten Son so that we might be restored unto Him and come to know Him intimately.

Then, in the New Testament the Father sent Jesus to redeem us unto Himself, and for Jesus to reveal the Father to us, to reveal the will of God, the plan of God, and the purposes of God to us. Praise God! What a mighty God!

Unified with the Godhead

Now if you truly want that intimate relationship with God the Father which I have described, here's how you can obtain it. It comes by worshipping Him in spirit and in truth. That includes seeking Him daily through His Word – meditating upon it and speaking it out – praising Him for the great and mighty things He has done, developing your prayer life, which is having communion with Him. All of these things will cause you to have that intimate relationship with God.

In John 17:21 we see that Jesus describes our union with the Father and with Him. *That they all may be one, as You, Father, are in Me, and I in You; that they also may be one in Us, that the world may believe that You sent Me.*

> **"That they all may be one, as You, Father, are in Me, and I in You; that they also may be one in Us . . ." (John 17:21).**

The question now is to you! Are you truly hungry for this intimate relationship with the Father? Then I suggest that you make the decision to spend quality time with Him daily. The end result will be that you will indeed

> **Are you truly hungry for an intimate relationship with the Father?**

acquire that ecstatic and euphoric *ginosko* relationship with Him. The choice is yours!

Chapter 7

Knowing God the Son

Jesus is the Son of God. The Bible tells us, *For God so loved the world that He gave His only begotten Son, that whoever believes in Him should not perish but have everlasting life* (John 3:16).

Luke 19:10 says, *For the Son of Man has come to seek and to save that which was lost.*

Jesus is 100 percent God and 100 percent man. He is the Christ, the Messiah, the Anointed One of God, who has come to save the world.

John 1:1 says, *In the beginning was the Word, and the Word was with God, and the Word was God.* And John 1:14 says, *And the Word became flesh and dwelt among us, and we beheld His glory, the glory as of the only begotten of the Father, full of grace and truth.*

So we see that Jesus is the living Word. He is the Word made flesh. In heaven He is actually called The Word. In order to have an intimate relationship with Jesus, we must have intimate time in the Word each day. Jesus is revealed to us as we study and meditate and pray His Word. The Holy Spirit gives us revelation of Jesus through the Word. He confirms the Word.

> **Jesus is the living Word . . . He is revealed to us as we study and meditate and pray His Word.**

Religious people have never accepted Jesus' deity. They believe that He was a prophet, a good man, even a miracle worker, but they have never believed or confessed Him as Lord. Yet He is God the Son.

Jesus came to earth in the form of a man and emptied Himself in order to live an intimate life with God and fulfill God's plan for humanity, the mighty plan of salvation. As we observe the life of Jesus by studying the Word of God, and accept the signs and wonders and miracles that He accomplished while on earth, we begin to have a picture of Him in His fullness.

As we identify with Him through His death, burial, and resurrection as the Sacrificial Lamb who was sacrificed from the foundation of the world for us, we begin to enter into that intimate relationship with Him.

This intimate relationship begins when we accept Jesus as Lord and have that born-again experience which He provided. This relationship continues as we begin to receive the promises that He paid for on the cross, which are salvation, eternal life, healing and wholeness, prosperity, protection, and His divine presence.

> **As we identify with Jesus Christ through His death, burial, and resurrection . . . we begin to enter into that intimate relationship with Him.**

All that He sacrificed His life for is ours as we press into that intimate relationship with Him.

> **All that He sacrificed His life for is ours as we press into that intimate relationship with Him.**

This is what Paul was crying out for in *His hunger and quest for God – to know Him in His fullness.*

Paul's Ephesians 1 Prayer

In studying the Word of God, the Scriptures tell us of Paul's prayers to know Him.

Paul prays in Ephesians 1:17-20:

17 *That the God of our Lord Jesus Christ, the Father of glory, may give to you the spirit of wisdom and revelation in the knowledge of Him,*

18 *the eyes of your understanding being enlightened; that you may know what is the hope of His calling, what are the riches of the glory of His inheritance in the saints,*

19 *and what is the exceeding greatness of His power toward us who believe, according to the working of His mighty power*

20 *which He worked in Christ when He raised Him from the dead and seated Him at His right hand in the heavenly places.*

Paul is praying that God, the Father of our Lord Jesus Christ, the Father of glory, may give unto us the spirit of wisdom and revelation in the knowledge of Him [Jesus]. Verse 18 says, *The eyes of your understanding being enlightened; that you may know what is the hope of His calling, what are the riches of the glory of His inheritance in the saints.* One translation says, *That we may be flooded with the light of who Jesus is and know His purpose and His calling.*

Verse 19 tells us that we should know the *exceeding greatness of His power toward us who believe, according to the working of His mighty power.* Verse 20 continues, *Which He worked in Christ when He raised Him* [Jesus] *from the dead. . . .*

You see, Paul is praying that we would have an intimate relationship with Jesus, that we would know Him in His fullness, including in His power and in His resurrection.

We can know the exceeding greatness of God's power toward us.

Paul's Ephesians 3 Prayer

In Ephesians 3:16-20 Paul prays:

16   *That He would grant you, according to the riches of His glory, to be strengthened with might through His Spirit in the inner man,*

17 *that Christ may dwell in your hearts through faith; that you, being rooted and grounded in love,*

18 *may be able to comprehend with all the saints what is the width and length and depth and height —*

19 *to know the love of Christ which passes knowledge; that you may be filled with all the fullness of God.*

20 *Now to Him who is able to do exceedingly abundantly above all that we ask or think, according to the power that works in us.*

In these scriptures, Paul is asking God to grant us according to the riches of His glory, to be strengthened with might through His Spirit in the inner man (v. 16), that Christ [the Anointed One of God and His anointing] may dwell in our hearts through faith, that we being rooted and grounded in love (v. 17) may be able to understand the width, the length, the depth, and the height (v. 18),

"To know the love of Christ which passes knowledge; that you may be filled with all the fullness of God" (Ephesians 3:19).

to know the love of Christ which surpasses knowledge and to be filled with all the fullness of God (v. 19). Verse 20 says, [He] *is able to do exceedingly abundantly above all that we ask or think according to the power that works in us.*

We are strengthened with might through God's Spirit in our inner man.

Paul's Colossians 1 Prayer

In Colossians 1:9-14 Paul prays,

God is able to do exceedingly abundantly above all that we ask or think according to the power that works in us.

9   *For this reason we also, since the day we heard it, do not cease to pray for you, and to ask that you may be filled with the knowledge of His will in all wisdom and spiritual understanding;*

10   *that you may walk worthy of the Lord, fully pleasing Him, being fruitful in every good work and increasing in the knowledge of God;*

11   *strengthened with all might, according to His*

glorious power, for all patience and longsuffering with joy;

12   *giving thanks to the Father who has qualified us to be partakers of the inheritance of the saints in the light.*

We are being filled with the knowledge of His will in all wisdom and spiritual understanding.

13   *He has delivered us from the power of darkness and conveyed us into the kingdom of the Son of His love,*

14   *in whom we have redemption through His blood, the forgiveness of sins.*

Paul is saying in verses 9 and 10, *[I] do not cease to pray for you, and to ask that you may be filled with the knowledge of His will in all wisdom and spiritual understanding; that you may walk worthy of the Lord, fully pleasing Him, being fruitful in every good work and increasing in the knowledge of God* [increasing in an intimate relationship with Jesus].

Paul continues to pray in verse 11, *[We are] strengthened with all might, according to His glorious power, for all patience and longsuffering with joy.*

Verse 13 tells us that we have been delivered from the power of darkness and transferred into the Kingdom of the Son of His love. Finally, verse 14 tells

> **"That you may walk worthy of the Lord, fully pleasing Him. . ." (Colossians 1:10).**

us that we are redeemed through Jesus' blood, and our sins have been forgiven. Praise God! What a mighty God!

Paul's Prayers Belong to Us

Paul's New Testament prayers belong to us. Therefore, we can pray these prayers each day for ourselves and others, and God will grant us that intimate relationship with Him. Paul is praying that Jesus be revealed in us and to us in a very intimate way

> **We have been delivered from the power of darkness and transferred into the Kingdom of the Son of His love.**

and that His plans and purposes be established for us.

Many have come to the Lord Jesus Christ, God the Son, and received Him as their Savior, but there's much, much more to knowing God the Son. We need to know Him as Lord and Master and have Him intimately involved in every area of our lives. We begin to know Him as Lord and Master in trusting Him in every situation that we face in life. Our utmost goal then is to have that intimate relationship with Him

Jesus is revealed in us and to us in a very intimate way.

and to reverence Him as Lord and Master.

Jesus Reveals Himself to Me

I couldn't catch my breath. Even with the oxygen mask on, I couldn't breathe. I was having congestive heart failure, and I was a hair's breath from going home to be with the Lord. I cried out, "Jesus, where are You? I want to see You face-to-face right now. What's going on?"

Instantly, Jesus walked straight towards me. He gave me a bear hug. His face was like a brilliant ball of light. He was like a glistening figure. His garment was glowing like white satin. The only thing I could see physically was His feet. He was wearing handmade sandals. He said, "Peace, son. I'm here." Then He said, "Sit down here. I want to talk to you." We sat on a wrought-iron bench. I was enthralled with the flowers. As I stepped on them, they popped right back up again. I couldn't crush them or hurt them in any way by walking on them.

Jesus said, "These doctors will help you, but they can't heal you. My Word will heal you. . . ."

Jesus continued, "You can't come yet. Your work is not finished." When He hugged me it felt like I was in a helium balloon. It was an awesome experience of peace. I kept thinking of Isaiah 26:3 KJV — *Thou wilt keep him in perfect peace, whose mind is stayed on thee. . . .*

Jesus said, "These doctors will help you, but they can't heal you. My Word will heal you. Go home, turn off the TV and everything else that will distract you, and get in My Word." That's exactly what I did!

Jesus added, "I heard you say that you have meditated upon Isaiah 26:3 fifty million times, especially in the dentist's office! Don't you think that's an exaggeration? But that's not a bad idea though. Meditating on My healing scriptures will heal you!"

He also said, "Your sister is pulling on the hem of My garment every day on your behalf. She is just as persistent here with Me as she was on earth. She wants you to finish your course."

I asked Jesus, "Can You give me scripture on that?" He gave me Hebrews 12:1: *Therefore we also, since we are surrounded by so great a cloud of witnesses, let us lay aside every weight, and the sin which so easily ensnares us, and let us run with endurance the race that is set before us.*

Jesus asked me, "Haven't you heard of the great cloud of witnesses in Hebrews 12? Your sister is one of these witnesses. What do you think your loved ones do up here? They pray with Me every day to help you fulfill your course. There are many things your sister told you to do that you haven't done yet. One of them is to write this book."

Then, in the snap of a finger, He was gone. He left me in perfect peace!

I was out of Intensive Care in two days. I had some serious heart damage, but Jesus said, "You don't know and understand My love for you, because if you did, you would receive your new heart now." I did receive the brand-new heart that God provided for me.

Pursuing Your Relationship with Jesus the Son

Are you hungry for Jesus? Are you hungry to know Him? If you want an intimate relationship with God the Son, read and study God's Word and ask the Holy Spirit to give you revelation and intimacy with Him.

Revelation by the Holy Spirit, daily meditating in the Word of God (particularly in the New Testament), studying the life of Christ Jesus, and maintaining a consistent prayer life, are ways to develop an intimate relationship with God the Son.

Chapter 8

Knowing God the Holy Spirit

The Holy Spirit is the third Person of the Godhead. He is God Almighty. He is the power of God and the presence of God. He is not to be thought of as just the power, the presence, or an influence. He is not a dove or any other symbol. He is a Person. Therefore, being the third Person of the Godhead, we need to know and have an intimate relationship with Him.

> **The Holy Spirit is not a dove or any other symbol. He is a Person – the third Person of the Godhead.**

Within this chapter we will endeavor to describe and to seek Him out so that we might have an intimate relationship with the Holy Spirit.

Jesus says in Luke 24:49, *Behold, I send the Promise of My Father upon you; but tarry in the city of Jerusalem until you are endued with power from on high.*

Since the Holy Spirit was fully poured out on the day of Pentecost, then He is fully here today.

So what Jesus foretold in the above reference occurred in the Upper Room on the day of Pentecost. On that day, according to Acts 1:8 and Acts 2:1-4, the Holy Ghost was fully poured out [and He is fully here today]. The subsequent events of the book of Acts prove the power, the influence, and the Person of the Holy Spirit. He was not only available to the first century Church, but He is available to the Church today and to each believer individually on a personal and intimate basis.

There is much, much more to our relationship with the Holy Spirit.

We first come in contact with the Person of the Holy Spirit in the new birth. He is the One who draws us to God and converts and transforms us unto Jesus. But this is only an initial experience with the Holy Spirit. There is much, much more. As I mentioned previously, in the book of Acts, chapters 1 and 2, there is a subsequent experience with the Holy Spirit — we must be baptized [immersed] in Him in order to have that personal relationship.

The Indwelling Life-Giving Spirit

In further looking at the Scriptures, we see the indwelling presence of the Holy Spirit. First Corinthians 6:19-20 says, *Or do you not know that your body is the temple of the Holy Spirit who is in you, whom you have from God, and you are not your own? For you were bought at a price; therefore glorify God in your body and in your spirit, which are God's.*

> **"Your body is the temple of the Holy Spirit . . ." (1 Corinthians 6:19).**

Romans 8:11 says, *But if the Spirit of Him who raised Jesus from the dead dwells in you, He who raised Christ from the dead will also give life to your mortal bodies through His Spirit who dwells in you.*

If you are a believer, that life-giving Spirit dwells in you, and He will quicken and heal your mortal body as you stand upon God's Word. *It is the Spirit who gives life; the flesh profits nothing. The words that I speak to you are spirit, and they are life* (John 6:63).

The Spirit gives life. The words Jesus speaks are spirit and life.

So you see, the Holy Spirit dwells within us. We are the temple of the Holy Spirit. We need to acknowledge that fact and act accordingly.

Imagine, the mighty power of God, the Holy Spirit, lives within you and me! Hallelujah! This is all the more reason we should get to know Him intimately.

Attributes of the Holy Spirit

Using John, chapters 14, 15, and 16 AMP as our reference, we will describe the attributes of the Holy Spirit, who He is, and what He wants to be to you.

Imagine, the mighty power of God, the Holy Spirit, lives in you and me!

The Holy Spirit is the Comforter, the Counselor, the Helper, the Intercessor, the

Advocate, the Strengthener, the Standby, and the Spirit of Truth. (John 14:16-17.) He is all of these things to you as you believe in Him and cultivate that intimate relationship with Him. He is none of these things to you if you do not cultivate that relationship with Him. His potential is always available, but it's up to you to tap into that intimate fellowship with Him.

> **The Holy Spirit is all of these things to us if we are cultivating an intimate relationship with Him — Comforter, Counselor, Helper, Intercessor, Advocate, Strengthener, Standby, and Spirit of Truth.**

We can have this intimate fellowship with the Person of the Holy Spirit on a regular and continual basis. But it is obtained through *trust and faith and by establishing daily communion with Him.*

The Word of God tells us in 2 Corinthians 13:14, *The grace of the Lord Jesus Christ, and the love of God, and the communion of the Holy Spirit be with you all. Amen.*

We see in this scripture that we are to have communion with the Holy Spirit. This word "communion" is the word *koinonia* in the Greek, and it means "an intimate and continuous fellowship."

An intimate and continuous fellowship is known as *koinonia* in the Greek.

As a result of having this fellowship with the Holy Spirit, we are to be led by the Holy Spirit. Romans 8:14-16 speaks of being led by the Holy Spirit and of the Holy Spirit bearing witness with our spirit. This is the predominant way Christians are to be led. Not by prophecy, although prophecy is good. Not by man's counsel, even though those counselors may be good and well meaning. But the

The predominant way Christians are led is by the Holy Spirit bearing witness with their spirit.

final authority is to be led by the Holy Spirit.

Charging Your Spiritual Battery

Now my question to you is, How can you be led by the Holy Spirit if you do not have this intimate relationship with Him? So many people are looking to prophets, pastors, evangelists, ministers, or other believers for the direction, the leading, and the wisdom of God instead of building this intimate relationship with the precious Holy Spirit and acquiring His leadership themselves.

In Jude 20, the Bible speaks of how you can build yourself up on your most holy faith and maintain that relationship with the Holy Spirit. It speaks of praying in the Holy Spirit. This word "building" means to charge like charging a battery in a car, so when you are praying in the Spirit, you are charging up your spiritual battery. This is what causes us to be sensitive to the Spirit and to follow His leading. It also causes us to have that intimate relationship with Him.

Are you looking for guidance or direction in your life? You must be led by the Holy Spirit.

When you are praying in the Spirit, you are charging up your spiritual battery. This helps build your intimate relationship with Him.

In Romans 8:26 we see that *the Spirit Himself makes intercession for us with groanings which cannot be uttered.* Verse 27 tells us that He searches the heart and knows the mind of God's Spirit, and He makes intercession for believers according to the will of God. Praise God for His precious Holy Spirit!

God the Holy Spirit is the Person of the Godhead who is here with us every day. He lives in us. God our Father and the Lord Jesus Christ sent Him to indwell us so that we might have Him as our Comforter, Leader, and Guide. We must know Him intimately and follow His leadership if we are going to be successful Christians, whose goal is to know God.

The Holy Spirit prays the perfect will of God for us.

Koinonia of the Spirit

Now how do we acquire knowledge of and fellowship with the Holy Spirit? It comes by reading God's Word, meditating upon it, praying daily in the Spirit, and asking the Holy Spirit to give us

We have fellowship with the Holy Spirit by reading and meditating upon God's Word, by praying in the Spirit, and by asking the Holy Spirit to give us revelation of the Word.

revelation of God's Word. The Holy Spirit always confirms the Word of God. Since He

The Holy Spirit always confirms the Word of God.

is a Person, we should talk to Him and ask Him to reveal Himself to us. He will reveal the Father and the Son, and He will establish that intimate personal relationship with us if we ask

Intimacy with the Holy Spirit is a life-changing experience.

Him and are hungry for Him.

My whole life and ministry have changed as a result of my daily relationship with the Person of the Holy Spirit. I highly recommend that you develop this fellowship *{koinonia}* of the Spirit in your own life daily.

Chapter 9

Building a Daily Lifestyle of Intimacy with God

Desiring intimacy with God and a daily relationship with Him is a lifestyle and, as such, it must be developed and worked at. It takes discipline to acquire this intimacy.

Intimacy with God is a lifestyle.

The Bible tells us that wise men still seek Him. We are to seek Him, and He may be found if we are diligent in our seeking. The Bible also tells us to seek Him early. Therefore, our morning time is a good time to seek Him. Your time to seek Him may vary due to your specific schedule, but God willingly wants to meet with you on a regular basis. All you need to do is to make quality time available to Him.

Hindrances to Building an Intimate Relationship

There are some hindrances to building an intimate relationship with God which must be dealt with. Things

Wise men still seek Him!

like offenses, negative thoughts, worry, fear, or sin. All of these, along with other things, such as

God wants to meet with you every day.

excessive work schedules, TV, and entertainment, can hinder your

intimate relationship with God. We must ask the Holy Spirit to reveal the hindrances to us and give us godly repentance. We must confess everything that is unpleasing to the Lord and cast our cares

Remove the hindrances to building an intimate relationship, such as excessive work schedules, TV, entertainment, etc.

upon Him before we can enter into this intimate relationship.

If you wonder why you haven't had this deeper relationship before, or maybe you've only had it occasionally, search your heart. Ask the Holy Spirit to reveal to you whatever

> **We must confess everything that is unpleasing to the Lord and cast our cares upon Him before we can enter into this intimate relationship.**

changes and/or adjustments need to be made so you can enjoy this intimacy with God.

Meditation

Previously, we talked about seeking God through a daily prayer time, Bible reading, and meditation upon His Word. What I mean by meditation is reading the Word and pondering it, thinking deeply

> **Search your heart and ask the Holy Spirit to reveal any adjustments you need to make.**

upon its content, muttering it under your breath, and speaking it forth so you can hear it. Ask the Holy Spirit to give you revelation of the Word you are reading so it will become life to you.

In addition to meditating on the Word of God, we need to meditate on who God is and consider His character and nature and all that He is and wants to be to us. We also need to meditate on Jesus our Lord and all that He accomplished on the cross through His death, burial, and resurrection. Then, we need to dwell on our covenant relationship with Him.

> Meditation is so important for an intimate relationship: Meditate the Word, think deeply upon it, speak it. Above all, consider God's character and nature and what Jesus has done for you.

Meditating on the things of God will cause us to have that intimate relationship with Him that we desire. Meditation of God's Word is a lost art that Christians need to practice on a regular basis.

> Meditation of God's Word is a lost art that we need to practice.

God the Father, the Son, and the Holy Spirit are always reaching out to us, so we need to take the time to respond and interact with them.

Praying in the Spirit

Another way of obtaining this intimate relationship is by praying in the Spirit. It's by revelation that the Holy Spirit establishes this relationship. He is the most important member of the Godhead to us as believers in that He reveals the Father and the Son to us.

> **Being still before God is also a lost art and needs to be reawakened in believers.**

The Word of God says, *Be still, and know that I am God* (Psalm 46:10). Being still before God is also a lost art and needs to be reawakened in believers. Many times in our prayer life we are always talking, and we never give God an opportunity to respond. We need to learn to be in His presence and to still our body, soul (which includes the mind, will, and emotions), and spirit, and listen with our spiritual ears for God to speak to us.

God is communicating with our spirit all the time, especially in those times when we are seeking Him. But we rarely get quiet or still enough to receive from Him.

Prayer is a two-way communication with God. And, as such, we should learn to be still before Him and be blessed by what He is saying to us. In these still moments, the Holy Spirit will reveal

> **We must learn to practice the presence of the Lord by getting quiet before Him.**

to us the will of God, the plan of God, and the purpose of God. He gives forth God's wisdom.

Waiting Upon the Lord

As we press forward to knowing and having an intimate relationship with God, we must consider waiting upon the Lord. **Waiting upon the Lord is a lost art to the Church and to believers today.**

> **Prayer is a two-way communication with God.**

As Christians today, we have such a busy lifestyle that either we don't have time or we don't take time to practice waiting upon the Lord.

To wait upon the Lord means to be still and know that He is God (Psalm 46:10). In other words, in our prayer time, we should not be speaking all the time. Learn to still your mind and body and just let God communicate with your spirit. Let Him speak to your heart.

> **Waiting upon the Lord is a lost art to the Church and to believers today.**

In these precious moments of intimacy, He will impart to you **wisdom, guidance, direction,** and **answers** for the very things for which you are seeking Him. This is why it is so vital to wait upon Him in your daily time of intimacy with Him.

Many times the Holy Spirit will bring a scripture up inside of you, or He will direct you to a scripture. God always speaks through His Word, and sometimes He will even speak audibly, if He chooses to do so. But for the most part, God's Spirit communicates with your spirit. This is one of the key ways we can have this intimate relationship with Him.

This type of relationship is also called waiting upon the Lord. However, waiting upon the Lord includes more than meditation and being still. It also includes worship and praise and practicing His presence. As a result of waiting upon the Lord, we renew our strength. The joy of the Lord becomes our strength. As His presence envelops us, we experience that intimate relationship.

Waiting upon the Lord includes . . . worship and praise and practicing His presence.

These are some very valuable and vital ways to establish an intimate relationship with Him.

If you are truly hungry for God, you need to establish a daily plan to seek Him that fits your schedule, and expect Him to meet you. Be consistent, be diligent, and He will reward you with intimate fellowship and relationship, for [God] *is a rewarder of those who diligently seek Him* (Hebrews 11:6).

If you are truly hungry for God, you need to establish a daily plan to seek Him.

Chapter 10

My Personal Intimate Relationship with God

I would like to share with you some insights into my personal intimate relationship with God that might help you in establishing your intimate relationship with Him. As I mentioned earlier, everyone's schedule may be different. Therefore, you must adapt the development of your intimate relationship with God to fit your lifestyle and schedule.

Adapt and establish a lifetime schedule for the development of your intimate relationship with God.

God spoke to my heart in the very beginning of the ministry, more than twenty years ago, to go and teach My people to *be doers of the word, and not hearers only*, not deceiving [themselves] (James 1:22). With that in mind, I would like to share with you some ways that you can apply these principles to your life for building your intimate relationship with God.

> **"Be doers of the Word, and not hearers only . . ."**
> **(James 1:22).**

Each morning when I rise, the first thing I do after washing my face is go back to my bed and throw the pillow on the floor, kneel, and begin to worship and praise God the Father, the Son, and the Holy Spirit with upraised hands and a heart full of thanksgiving. I worship the Father and the Son for at least five minutes. Then, I ask the Holy Spirit to be my Helper, my Strengthener, my Comforter, and my Counselor for that day. I also ask for God's wisdom for the day.

After worshipping Him at least five minutes, I have my daily reading of the Word and meditation. You should have a daily Bible-reading program that's at least ten to fifteen minutes of quality time a day. God will speak to you in these special moments through His Word and by His Spirit.

My time in the Word extends beyond ten or fifteen minutes, but since I am a minister of the gospel, I need to spend much more time in the Word and in prayer. However, even with a busy schedule, you should be able to spend at least ten minutes or so in the Word. If you spend the first five minutes in worship and then ten minutes in the Word, that is the most valuable fifteen minutes that you can spend in your day. Everyone should be able to give God at least fifteen minutes of his or her day.

Having a daily Bible reading program is a must. God will speak to you in these special moments.

After my worship time and time in the Word, I put on a praise tape and begin to worship and praise God and speak His Word [His promises] back to Him while I am exercising, which amounts to about fifteen minutes. Exercising, of course, is optional, but it will greatly help you mentally and physically.

Fifteen minutes a day with God is the most valuable time of your day.

God is interested in the whole man, and He wants to bless you — spirit, soul, and body. He may even speak to you about your health and how to make changes for the better, including how to receive and maintain your healing. My time with God is a very special time for me.

Now some of you may not have enough time, so what I suggest is that you put on a praise or Scripture tape in your vehicle and worship God and listen to His Word as you're going to work. Write down one scripture on a 3 x 5 card and meditate on that scripture all day long. Put it on your refrigerator or on your sun visor. Continue to meditate and speak out the scripture(s) that you need for your life, and it will become life to you. This is how to build your intimate relationship with God.

Practicing God's presence is a goal of mine. Therefore, I try to keep my mind stayed upon Him because I trust in Him. (See Isaiah 26:3.) Practicing the presence of God is a vital way to have an intimate relationship with Him.

Practicing the presence of God is a vital way to have an intimate relationship with Him.

Ephesians 5:18 tells us, *Be filled with the Spirit.* The Greek states, "Be being filled as a continuous process." Verses 19 and 20 say, *Speaking to one another* [or among yourselves] *in psalms and hymns and spiritual songs, singing and making melody in your heart to the Lord, giving thanks always for all things to God the Father in the name of our Lord Jesus Christ.* [Note: Give thanks *in* all things, not *for* all things, such as the devil's attacks.] These are some very practical ways you can practice the presence of God.

Give thanks *in* all things, not *for* all things.

Fear [or Reverence] the Lord

One final thought relates to the fear of the Lord. Having the fear of the Lord means to have reverence for God. It is not to be afraid of Him, but to reverence Him with a holy awe, for He is God Almighty, and He is to be reverenced above all.

The fear of the Lord is another lost art in the church and among believers today.

The fear of the Lord is a holy awe or reverence for Him and for His presence, His manifestation, and His mighty working power! Many in the church today, especially in the times when the

Holy Spirit is moving, are distracted and even irreverent for the things of God. Many never enter into reverence in their private prayer time with God. So they wonder why they don't have that intimate relationship with Him.

Practicing reverence and holy awe of the Lord will insure your intimacy with Him.

Having the fear of the Lord means . . . to reverence Him with a holy awe.

We are to cry out to Him, **Holy, Holy, Holy is the Lord God Almighty,** and give glory and honor and reverence to the Lamb who sits on the Throne.

It is my sincere desire that you will build a personal intimate relationship with God. My prayer for you then is that this book has created a hunger in your heart and a stir in your soul to know God and to have an intimate relationship with Him!

I pray that you will be abundantly blessed as you continue to pursue Him. Amen.

The Beginning

About the Author

As a young man Anthony LuPardo was quite successful in the business world. While in his twenties, he managed a multi-million dollar operation in Europe, which resulted in an additional $20 million contract for the company. Although he did not have a personal relationship with God and didn't possess a hunger for Him, Brother Anthony attended church regularly and cried out to God for wisdom and direction.

But there was always something lacking in his life and an emptiness inside that plagued him. With his marriage failing and his financial status diminishing, Brother Anthony one day found himself contemplating suicide. Knowing there had to be something more to life, he cried out to God in desperation. Like the apostle Paul, Brother Anthony began searching for an intimate relationship with God, but he didn't know how to obtain it.

Then the Lord brought Christian television across his path, The Trinity Broadcasting Network (TBN), and through the ministry of Paul and Jan Crouch, Brother Anthony received Jesus Christ as his Lord and Savior.

Brother Anthony was born again, and his life changed dramatically. While in Israel with TBN, he and his wife Gina were baptized in the Jordan River and received the power of God into their lives through baptism in the Holy Spirit.

Since that time Brother Anthony has completed television ministry certification, working both for TBN and Oral Roberts Ministries in television production and management.

He has completed Bible college and is a gifted teacher of God's Word. He also moves in the prophetic realm. He has been in the ministry for more than twenty years.

Several years ago while Brother Anthony was in a coma and within a hair's breath of death following congestive heart failure, Jesus appeared to him and said, "You can't come yet. Your work is not finished."

"One of the things He spoke to me about specifically," says Brother Anthony, "was the publication of this book. He said that the publication of this book on having an intimate relationship with Him was a large part of my life and ministry and is greatly needed by the Body of Christ. He has since healed me and is fulfilling His promises in my life. Praise God for His faithfulness. To God be all the glory!"

Brother Anthony and his wife Gina travel throughout the United States and in foreign countries teaching the Word of God through seminars about building an intimate relationship with God. Their *Power for Living Seminars* address daily living, walking in the Spirit, and building a daily relationship with Him.

Since Brother Anthony and Sister Gina have obtained their doctorates in naturopathic health and counseling, they also teach *Better Health for Better Living Seminars* to the Body of Christ.

Their utmost desire is to be a blessing to all who are hungry for an intimate relationship with God.

If you desire to have Brother Anthony minister, you may write or call or E-mail:

Jesus for Life Ministries
P. O. Box 54714
Tulsa, Oklahoma 74155 U.S.A.
918/748-1777
jflministries@cfaith.com

Invitation to Relationship

Your Personal Commitment

Dr. Anthony is deeply concerned for your life and your intimate relationship with God.

If you have never come to God or made Jesus the Lord of your life, this is your moment to do so.

Just pray this prayer:

Father, I come to You in the name of Jesus. You said in Your Word in Romans 10:9,10, *If you confess with your mouth the Lord Jesus and believe in your heart that God has raised Him from the dead, you will be saved. For with the heart one believes unto righteousness, and with the mouth confession is made unto salvation.*

Father, I believe that Jesus died for my sins to save my soul. Jesus, come into my heart and be the Lord of my life. Fill me with Your Holy Spirit. I receive You now. Thank You, Father. Amen.

If you prayed this prayer, please contact us at jflministries@cfaith.com and we will send you a free gift. We love you and appreciate you.

Remain blessed,

Dr. Anthony J. LuPardo

Other Materials for Building Intimacy with God

In my hunger for intimacy with God, these are some of the books that assisted me in drawing near and building an intimate relationship with Him. They may be helpful to you in your quest for your intimate relationship with God. Many more books and materials are available as well. I have been so blessed to have had exposure not only to these books but to many leading men and women in ministry who helped create that hunger in me. I am so thankful to God for everything He has used to draw me unto Himself. My fervent prayer is that the Holy Spirit will lead you and guide you in your hunger and quest for your intimate relationship with God.

Walking with God
by W. Phillip Keller
Fleming H. Revell Publishers

"Spiritual Hunger," "The God-Men,"
and Other Sermons
by John G. Lake
Edited by Gordon Lindsay
Christ for the Nations, Inc.

Good Morning, Holy Spirit
by Benny Hinn
Thomas Nelson Publishers

Presenting the Holy Spirit
by Fuschia Pickett
Creation House

Placed in His Glory
by Fuschia Pickett
Charisma House

The Practice of the Presence of God
by Brother Lawrence
Whitaker House

Notes

Notes

Notes

_____

_____

_____

_____

_____

_____

_____

_____

_____

_____

_____

_____

_____

_____

_____

_____

Notes

Notes

Notes

Notes

Notes